Ted Richard

Ancient Civilizations

FOR KIDS

Uncovering the Secrets of Our World's First Cultures

Contents

Introduction to the Ancient World

What does "Ancient" mean?

"Ancient" is a word we use to describe something very, very old—so old that it existed thousands of years ago! The Ancient World began about 3000 years before people started counting time as we do today and lasted until around 500 AD.

This was a time when the world looked very different from how it looks now. There were no cars, computers, or tall skyscrapers. But the people in these times were incredibly smart and creative. They built amazing cities, invented clever tools, and learned so much about the world around them.

When we talk about the "Ancient World," we mean special groups of people called "civilizations" who lived in big regions and created unique ways of living. Some of the most famous ancient civilizations include the Egyptians, who built the Great Pyramids; the Greeks, who told stories of powerful gods and heroes; and the Romans, who built roads and aqueducts that helped people travel and get clean water.

In the ancient world, people came up with ideas about how to live together in cities, share food and goods, and even write down stories. Some of the things they created, like letters, numbers, and buildings, still influence our lives today.

So, learning about the ancient world is like going on a time-travel adventure to discover how life used to be and to find out what amazing things were invented back then!

Where and When Did Ancient Civilizations Live?

Ancient civilizations began thousands of years ago in different parts of the world. They developed in places where people learned to grow food, build homes, and work together in large groups. Many of these civilizations began near rivers, which provided water for farming and drinking.

Let's take a look at some of the main areas where these ancient civilizations began:

Egypt: In Africa, the ancient Egyptians lived along the Nile River, which gave them water for farming and made their land very fertile. They started building their civilization around 3100 BC. Egypt became known for its huge pyramids, impressive temples, and powerful pharaohs.

Mesopotamia: This civilization started even earlier, around 4000 BC, between the Tigris and Euphrates Rivers, in a place called the "Fertile Crescent." Today, this area is mostly in Iraq. Mesopotamia is where people invented some of the first writing, laws, and cities.

China: Ancient China began along the Yellow River around 2000 BC. Chinese civilization brought many inventions, like paper, silk, and the compass, which later spread to other parts of the world.

Greece: Around 800 BC, the ancient Greeks began their civilization near the Mediterranean Sea. Greece is famous for its myths about gods and heroes, the start of democracy, and the Olympic Games, which people still celebrate today.

Rome: The Roman civilization started around 750 BC in what is now Italy. The Romans created a vast empire that included much of Europe, parts of Africa, and Asia. They built roads, aqueducts, and amazing buildings, like the Colosseum.

The Maya: In Central America, the Maya civilization developed around 2000 BC and became especially powerful around 250 AD. They lived in parts of what are now Mexico, Guatemala, and Belize. The Maya were skilled in astronomy and math, creating a complex calendar system and impressive pyramids.

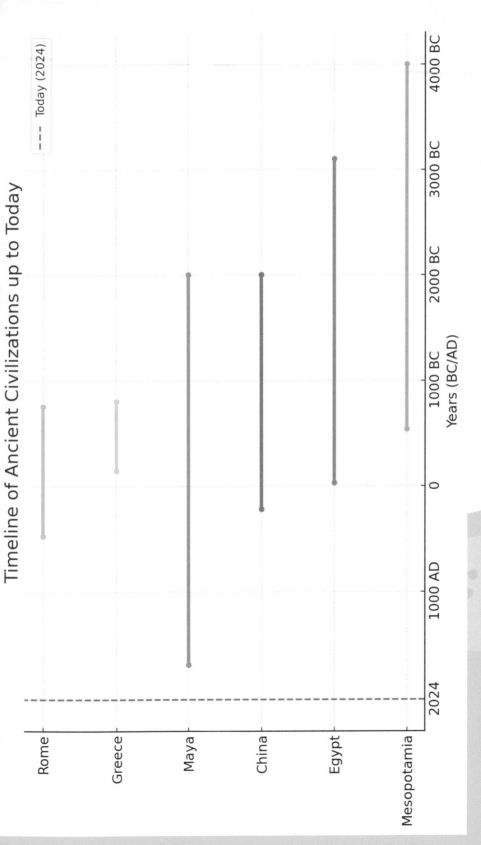

Timeline of Ancient Civilizations up to Today

"BC stands for 'Before Christ,' marking years before the birth of Jesus, while AD stands for 'Anno Domini,' a Latin term meaning 'In the Year of Our Lord,' which marks years after his birth."

Why Is It Exciting to Learn About Them?

Learning about ancient civilizations is like stepping into a time machine to explore a world full of mysteries, amazing inventions, and stories that helped shape who we are today. These civilizations built massive pyramids, created languages, and discovered things about the stars and planets—all without the technology we have now. They invented ways of writing, counting, and building that still influence us.

Exploring their stories shows us how creative and clever people were, even thousands of years ago. By learning about how they lived, what they believed, and what they made, we can better understand how people faced challenges and solved problems long before modern tools existed. Plus, their myths and legends are full of heroes, gods, and epic adventures, bringing history to life in a fun and exciting way!

The Egyptians
The People by the Nile

Egypt is here

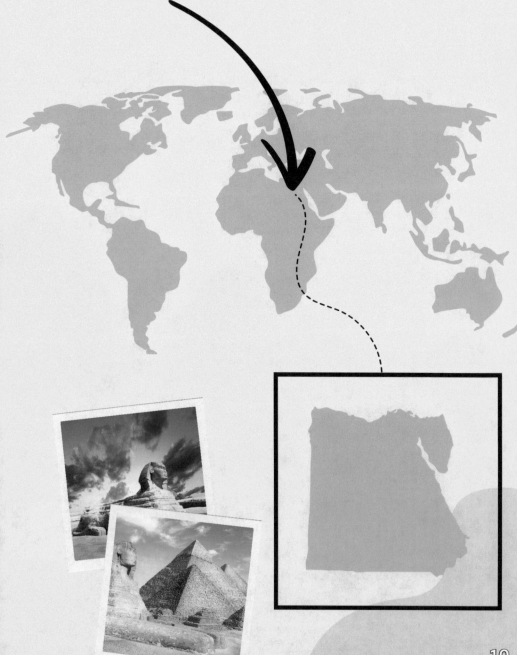

Life by the Nile: Water, Food, and the Pharaoh

The Nile River was like a lifeline for ancient Egypt. Flowing through the middle of a dry desert, the Nile provided water for drinking, farming, and travel. Each year, the river would overflow, covering the nearby land with rich, dark soil. This soil was perfect for growing crops, which allowed the Egyptians to have plenty of food. They grew wheat, barley, and vegetables, and even had room for fruit trees!

The Nile wasn't just important for food—it was also a natural highway. People traveled along the river in boats, trading goods like pottery, cloth, and grain. The Nile connected different parts of Egypt, making it easier for people to communicate and share ideas.

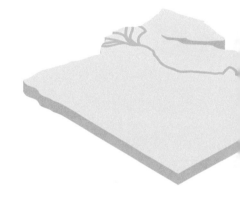

At the top of Egyptian society was the Pharaoh, the powerful ruler of Egypt. Egyptians believed the Pharaoh was like a god on Earth and that he had the power to keep Egypt safe and prosperous. The Pharaoh made important decisions about farming, building, and trade. Many Pharaohs built huge temples and tombs, like the famous pyramids, to honor themselves and the gods.

Thanks to the Nile, Egypt became one of the strongest and most advanced civilizations of its time. The river's water, the Pharaoh's leadership, and the hard work of the people allowed Egypt to thrive for thousands of years.

This image shows the iconic golden mask of Pharaoh Tutankhamun.

The Pyramids: Secrets of the Great Structures

The pyramids of Egypt are some of the most amazing buildings ever made. They were built thousands of years ago as tombs for the Pharaohs, who were both kings and believed to be like gods. The most famous pyramid, the Great Pyramid of Giza, was built for Pharaoh Khufu and is one of the Seven Wonders of the Ancient World.

Building these huge structures took many years, thousands of workers, and heavy stone blocks that weighed as much as an elephant! The ancient Egyptians didn't have machines, so they used ramps, ropes, and their own strength to lift and place the stones. The workers were skilled and proud of their work, living in nearby villages and getting good food to stay strong.

Why were the pyramids built in this special shape? The Egyptians believed that the pyramid's shape, pointing to the sky, helped the Pharaoh's soul rise up to join the gods. Inside, they placed rooms with treasures, food, and other things the Pharaoh would need in the afterlife.

Even today, scientists are still learning about the secrets of the pyramids, like hidden rooms and mysterious markings. The pyramids show us how talented the ancient Egyptians were and why these great structures are still remembered as one of history's greatest achievements.

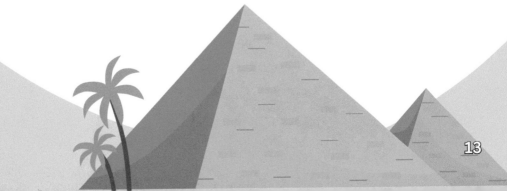

Gods and Stories: Isis, Osiris, and Horus

The ancient Egyptians believed in many gods and told amazing stories about them. These gods were powerful and could control nature, protect people, and guide them in the afterlife. Three of the most important gods were Isis, Osiris, and Horus, who were all part of the same family.

Isis: Isis was a loving and magical goddess who protected Egypt. She was known for her healing powers and great wisdom. Egyptians believed that Isis could help people in need and guide them to a happy afterlife. She is often shown with wings and was admired for her bravery and love for her family.

Osiris: Osiris was the god of the afterlife and the husband of Isis. He was a kind and wise king who taught people about farming and fairness. According to legend, Osiris was killed by his jealous brother, Set. But Isis used her magic to bring him back to life, which made Egyptians believe that death was not the end but a new beginning.

Horus: Horus was the son of Isis and Osiris and was often shown with the head of a falcon. After his father was killed, Horus fought Set to win back the throne. The Eye of Horus became a symbol of protection and healing. Egyptians believed that Horus was a strong protector and the god of the sky.

The stories of Isis, Osiris, and Horus taught the ancient Egyptians important lessons about loyalty, love, and the journey of life and death. They believed these gods watched over them and could be asked for protection, wisdom, and strength. These tales made the religion of ancient Egypt rich and full of inspiration, helping people feel connected to the gods and their world.

FUN FACT

Mummies: The ancient Egyptians believed that when someone died, their spirit would need a well-preserved body for the afterlife. To get ready for this journey, they created a special process called mummification. During this process, they carefully dried the body, wrapped it in linen, and placed it in a decorated coffin. Mummies were often buried with food, clothes, and treasures to help them in the afterlife. Mummification could take up to 70 days and was mostly done for pharaohs and rich people. Because of this careful process, some mummies have lasted thousands of years, giving us a chance to learn more about ancient Egypt!

The ancient Egyptians had their own special writing system called hieroglyphics. Unlike our alphabet, hieroglyphics used hundreds of symbols that stood for sounds, words, or ideas. Some symbols looked like animals, while others were simple shapes or objects.

The Egyptians used hieroglyphics to write down important events, tell stories, and decorate temples and tombs. They even wrote on a kind of paper made from papyrus plants. For many years, people couldn't read hieroglyphics until the Rosetta Stone was found in 1799. This stone had the same writing in three different languages, which helped experts finally figure out how to read hieroglyphics!

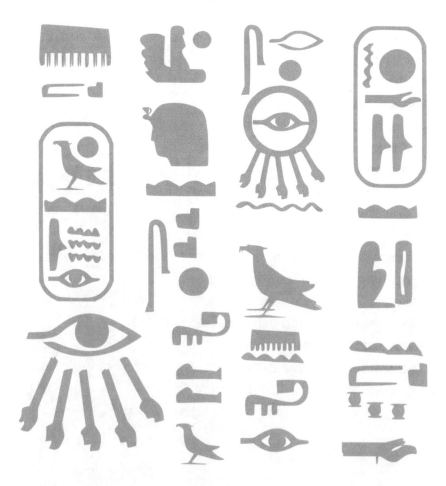

FAMOUS

Cleopatra, the Last Queen of Egypt

Cleopatra VII was the last queen of ancient Egypt and is remembered for being smart, brave, and a great leader. She was born in 69 BC and came from a powerful family that ruled Egypt after the time of Alexander the Great. Cleopatra stood out because she could speak many languages and was very clever.

Cleopatra was known for being highly intelligent and loved to learn about philosophy, literature, and science. When she became queen, Egypt faced many problems, and Rome was becoming very powerful. Cleopatra worked hard to make Egypt strong and keep it safe.

Cleopatra formed friendships with two important Roman leaders, Julius Caesar and later Mark Antony. These alliances helped her keep Egypt safe and strong. Cleopatra and Julius Caesar even had a son named Caesarion. After Caesar's death, Cleopatra became close to Mark Antony, and they had three children together. But their friendship with Rome made another leader, Octavian, very angry and led to a big battle.

In 31 BC, Cleopatra and her ally, Antony, were defeated by Octavian, who wanted to control Egypt. Antony was very sad about losing, and Cleopatra, not wanting to be taken prisoner, chose to stay loyal to her kingdom until the end. With Cleopatra's death, Egypt became part of the Roman Empire.

Even though Cleopatra is no longer with us, her story has been remembered for thousands of years. She is known as a queen who was smart, strong, and always did her best to protect her people. Her life has inspired many books, plays, and movies, showing that she was one of the most interesting leaders in history.

Cleopatra's story teaches us about bravery, intelligence, and the challenges of being a ruler in a time of great change.

This image depicts an ancient Egyptian wall carving featuring Queen Cleopatra alongside a pharaoh, surrounded by intricate hieroglyphs that highlight their regal status and connection to the gods.

The Greeks
Inventors and Storytellers

Greece is here

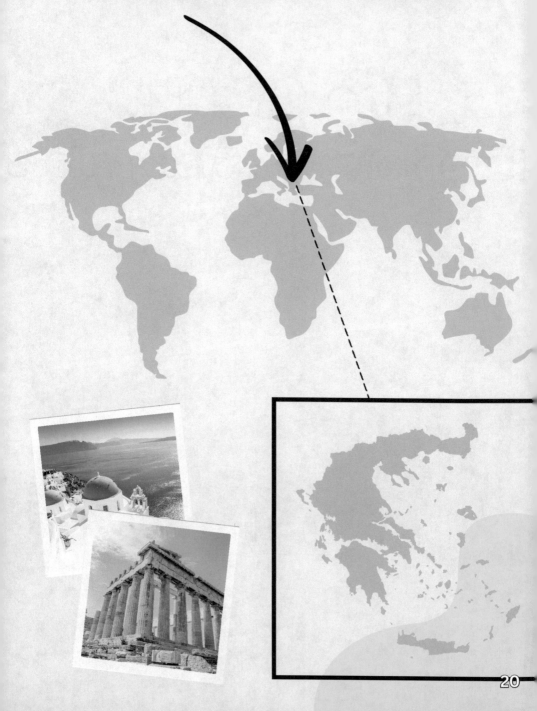

Daily Life in Athens and Sparta: How Did the Greeks Live?

In ancient Greece, life was different depending on where you lived. Two of the most famous cities, Athens and Sparta, had very different ways of life, but both were important in shaping Greek culture.

Athens: Life in Athens was all about learning, art, and democracy. People in Athens believed education was important, so boys went to school to study reading, writing, math, and sports. Girls usually stayed at home to learn how to take care of the house. Athens was special because it created the world's first democracy, where citizens could vote on important decisions. Athenians also loved the arts—they enjoyed watching plays, visiting beautiful temples, and making amazing sculptures.

Sparta: In Sparta, life was all about strength and discipline. Spartans were known as fierce warriors, and their main focus was on military training. From a young age, boys trained to become soldiers, learning to be brave and strong. Girls in Sparta also trained in sports to become healthy and strong mothers. Unlike Athens, where citizens could speak freely, Sparta had strict rules, and people were expected to follow orders without question. Spartans lived simply and didn't focus much on art or learning, as their main goal was to protect their city.

Though Athens and Sparta had different lifestyles, both cities played important roles in Greek culture. Athens gave us ideas about democracy and art, while Sparta showed the importance of discipline and bravery. Together, they created a powerful civilization that still inspires us today.

The Olympic Games: The Origin of Sports Competitions

The Olympic Games started over 2,700 years ago in ancient Greece, in a town called Olympia. These games were held every four years to honor Zeus, the king of the Greek gods. Athletes from different cities came to Olympia to show how strong, skilled, and brave they were.

The first Olympic Games had events like running, long jump, wrestling, and throwing the discus. One of the most exciting events was the chariot race, where drivers raced horses at high speeds. Winners of the games were given a wreath made of olive leaves, which was a special prize. These athletes were seen as heroes, and winning brought honor and respect to their city.

During the games, all wars and conflicts were paused so that people could travel safely to and from Olympia. This "Olympic Truce" showed how important the games were to the Greeks. The Olympic Games continued for hundreds of years until they were eventually stopped.

In 1896, the Olympics were revived as the modern Olympic Games, bringing together athletes from around the world. Today's Olympics may have many new events, but they still celebrate the same spirit of strength, competition, and unity that began in ancient Greece.

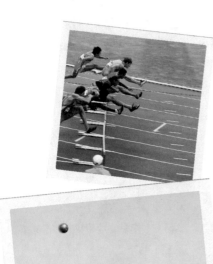

The ancient Greeks loved telling stories about their gods and heroes. These myths were full of adventure, bravery, and magic, and they explained the world around them. Three of the most famous figures in Greek mythology are Zeus, Hercules, and the story of the Trojan War.

Zeus

Zeus was the king of the gods and ruled from his throne on Mount Olympus. He was known for his power over thunder and lightning and was often shown holding a lightning bolt. Zeus was the most important of all the gods and kept order among them. He was wise but could be quick-tempered, especially if someone challenged his authority!

Hercules

Hercules, the son of Zeus, was one of the greatest heroes in Greek mythology. Known for his incredible strength, Hercules faced twelve difficult tasks, called the "Labors of Hercules." These included fighting fierce beasts, capturing a golden deer, and cleaning huge stables in a single day. His bravery and strength made him famous, and the Greeks admired him as a hero who overcame great challenges.

Statue of Hercules

The Trojan War

The Trojan War was a legendary battle between the Greeks and the city of Troy. It all started when Paris, a prince of Troy, took Helen, the queen of Sparta, back to Troy with him. This angered the Greeks, who set sail to Troy to bring Helen back. The war lasted for ten years and included many famous heroes, like Achilles and Odysseus.

To finally win, the Greeks used a clever trick called the "Trojan Horse"—a giant wooden horse hiding Greek soldiers inside. When the Trojans brought it into their city, the hidden soldiers came out at night, opened the gates, and ended the war.

Alexander the Great, the World Conqueror

Alexander the Great was one of the most famous and successful leaders in history. He was born in 356 BC in Macedonia (in present-day Greece) and was the son of King Philip II and Queen Olympias. Alexander was known for being very smart, ambitious, and a great military leader.

Alexander was taught by the famous philosopher Aristotle, who showed him subjects like science, philosophy, and literature. This education made Alexander curious and helped him become a strong leader. By the time he was 16, Alexander was already leading soldiers in battle.

When Alexander was 20, his father died, and he became the king of Macedonia. He quickly made sure his kingdom was safe and then set out to conquer the Persian Empire, which was the biggest empire at the time.

Alexander led his army on a journey that lasted over 10 years, traveling thousands of miles from Greece to Egypt, Persia, and even India. He won many battles, including the Battle of Issus and the Battle of Gaugamela, which helped him defeat King Darius III of Persia. In Egypt, Alexander was seen as a hero and was made a pharaoh. He also founded the city of Alexandria, which became famous for its culture and knowledge.

Alexander's army reached India, where he won a big battle against King Porus. But after many years of fighting, his soldiers were tired and wanted to go home, so Alexander turned back to Babylon.

Alexander died suddenly at the age of 32 in 323 BC. People aren't sure why he died, but it could have been from an illness. After his death, his huge empire was divided among his generals. Even though the empire didn't stay united, Alexander spread Greek culture and ideas everywhere he went, blending them with local customs.

Alexander the Great is remembered as a brilliant leader who never lost a battle. His journey changed history and connected the cultures of the East and West, leaving a legacy that is still remembered today.

Philosophy and Democracy: What Do They Mean?

The ancient Greeks came up with many ideas that changed the world, and two of the most important were philosophy and democracy.

Philosophy: Philosophy means "the love of wisdom." It is a way of thinking that asks big questions about life, like "What makes us happy?" or "What is fair?" Greek philosophers like Socrates, Plato, and Aristotle spent their time studying and talking about these questions. Socrates taught people to ask questions and think for themselves. Plato wrote about justice and how people can live well together, and Aristotle studied nature and science. These ideas encouraged people to think deeply, and they are still important today.

Democracy: Democracy is a type of government where people have the power to make decisions. In ancient Athens, democracy meant that citizens could vote on important issues and help choose leaders. Instead of being ruled by a king, Athenians gathered to talk about and vote on laws. This was one of the first democracies in history! Although only free men could vote, the idea of people having a say in their government was new and exciting, and it inspired many of the democracies we have today.

Philosophy and democracy from ancient Greece still shape the way we think and run our governments. The Greeks taught us to love learning, ask questions, and believe in the power of the people.

The Romans
Builders and World Rulers

Today's Rome is here

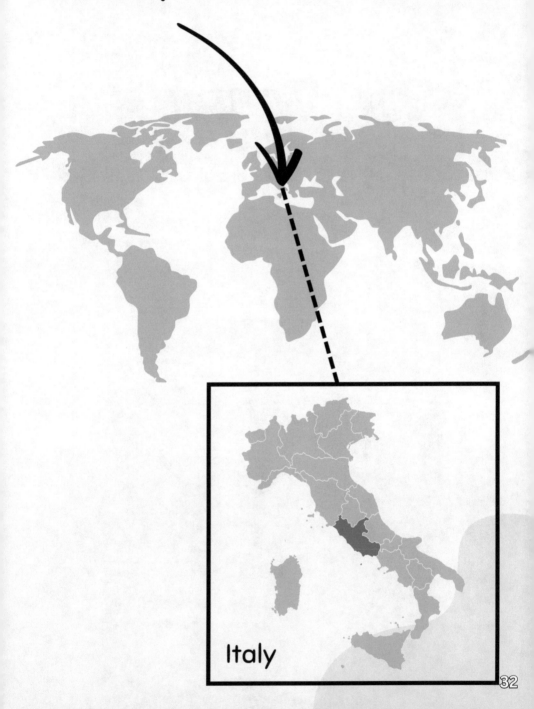

Italy

Life in Rome: Family, School, and Clothing

Daily life in ancient Rome was busy and organized. Family, school, and clothing were all important parts of Roman life.

Family: Family was very important to the Romans. The father, called the paterfamilias, was the head of the family and made big decisions. Roman families were often large, including grandparents, parents, children, and sometimes slaves. Family meals were special times for everyone to come together and share stories.

School: Education was important, especially for boys in wealthy families. Boys went to school to learn reading, writing, math, and public speaking. This helped them get ready for jobs in government or the army. Girls usually stayed at home to learn how to take care of the house. Rich families sometimes had private tutors, while others went to small local schools.

Clothing: Romans wore clothes that showed how important or rich they were. The main piece of clothing was the tunic, a long shirt tied at the waist. Men sometimes wore a toga over it, which was a large, draped cloth for special events. Women wore long dresses called stolas with a shawl called a palla over their shoulders. The colors and styles of clothing showed how wealthy a person was.

The influence of Roman clothing styles, particularly the tunic and toga, can still be seen today in modern fashion and formal attire. The classic design of long, flowing garments inspired robes worn by academics and judges in many countries, symbolizing status and authority, much like the toga did in ancient Rome. The idea of clothing representing status has persisted, with contemporary fashion using certain styles, fabrics, and colors to convey social and professional standing.

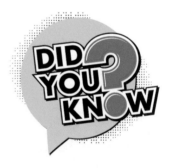

DID YOU KNOW?

The Colosseum and Gladiators: Entertainment in Ancient Rome

The Colosseum was one of the most amazing buildings in ancient Rome. It was a huge arena that could hold over 50,000 people, who came to watch exciting and sometimes dangerous shows.

One of the favorite events at the Colosseum was the gladiator games. Gladiators were fighters, often slaves or prisoners, who were trained to battle each other in front of loud, cheering crowds. They wore armor and used swords, shields, and spears. Sometimes, they even fought wild animals like lions and tigers, making the show even more thrilling. If a gladiator was very skilled and brave, he could win the admiration of the crowd and might even earn his freedom.

The games were carefully organized, and people from all parts of society came to watch, from the poorest citizens to the emperor himself. The audience would cheer for their favorite gladiators, and if a gladiator showed great skill, he could win the crowd's admiration—and sometimes even his freedom.

The Colosseum was more than just a place for entertainment; it was a symbol of Roman power and engineering. Its grand architecture, with rows of arches and high walls, was built to impress and endure. Today, the Colosseum stands as a reminder of the excitement and drama of ancient Rome, where people gathered to watch the bravery and strength of the gladiators.

The Roman Empire: How Far Did Rome Reach?

The Roman Empire was one of the biggest and most powerful empires in history. At its height, it stretched across Europe, parts of Asia, and North Africa. This meant that Roman culture, language, and ideas spread to many different places.

The Roman Empire started in Italy, but it grew as Roman armies, called legions, conquered new lands. These soldiers were well-trained and helped protect the empire. The Romans built roads, bridges, and cities to connect their vast lands, making travel and trade easier for everyone.

In Europe, the Roman Empire reached as far as present-day Spain, Portugal, and even parts of Britain and Germany. To the east, it included parts of modern Turkey and the Middle East. In Africa, the empire stretched across Egypt and along the northern coast.

The city of Rome was the heart of the empire. It was famous for its incredible buildings, like the Colosseum and the Roman Forum. The Romans brought their language, Latin, and their laws to the places they ruled. Many countries still use ideas from Roman laws today.

Even though the Roman Empire was powerful, it eventually faced problems and became weaker. By 476 AD, the Western Roman Empire fell, but the achievements of Rome and its vast empire are still remembered as one of the greatest accomplishments in history.

Roman Inventions: Roads, Aqueducts, and the Calendar

The Romans were not only great conquerors but also brilliant inventors who created amazing technologies that made life better and more organized. Some of their most important inventions include roads, aqueducts, and the calendar.

Roads: The Romans built a vast network of roads that connected cities and towns across the empire. These roads were so well made that some still exist today! Roman roads were built using layers of stone, gravel, and sand, making them strong and long-lasting. They allowed Roman legions to move quickly across the empire and helped merchants and travelers reach distant places. The saying "All roads lead to Rome" came from this impressive network, showing how central the city was to the entire empire.

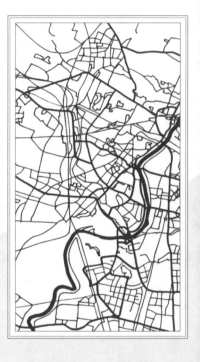

Aqueducts: Water was essential for the growing cities of Rome, and the Romans invented aqueducts to bring fresh water from faraway mountains and rivers into their cities. These aqueducts were stone structures that carried water over long distances, using gravity to keep the water flowing. With aqueducts, Roman cities had public baths, fountains, and indoor plumbing, which improved hygiene and made city life more comfortable. The most famous aqueducts,

like the Pont du Gard in France, still stand today as a testament to Roman engineering.

The Calendar: The Roman calendar has influenced the way we keep time today. Julius Caesar introduced the Julian calendar in 46 BC, which organized the year into 12 months and set the length of a year at 365 days, with an extra day added every four years (a leap year). This was a major improvement over older calendars, which were less accurate. The Julian calendar was later refined into the Gregorian calendar, which we still use today.

FAMOUS

Julius Caesar, the Mighty Roman

Julius Caesar was one of the most famous leaders of ancient Rome. He was born in 100 BC and was known for being brave and smart from a young age. Caesar wanted to make Rome bigger and stronger, and he went on many exciting adventures to achieve this.

A Powerful Leader: Julius Caesar became a great leader and conquered many lands for Rome, including all of Gaul (modern-day France). His soldiers admired him because he led them in thrilling battles and treated them well. One of his famous sayings, "Veni, vidi, vici," means "I came, I saw, I conquered," showing how quickly he could win victories.

One day, Caesar made an important decision. He led his army across the Rubicon River, even though it was forbidden. This meant he was ready to fight other Romans who wanted to stop him. This act started a big war, which Caesar won.

After winning the war, Caesar became the leader of Rome. He made new rules to help Rome and created a new calendar, which we still use in a similar way today. But some people were worried that Caesar was becoming too powerful and that Rome's freedom was at risk.

On March 15, 44 BC, Caesar was killed by some of his friends and enemies who thought that Rome should be free again. However, instead of bringing peace, his death led to more fighting, and eventually, Rome became an empire ruled by emperors.

Julius Caesar is remembered as a brave leader and clever strategist whose adventures and decisions changed Rome forever. His story teaches us that power can be exciting, but it can also be dangerous if it is not balanced.

FUN FACT

When Julius Caesar was a young man, he was once captured by pirates! The pirates asked for a ransom, but Caesar told them to ask for more because he thought he was worth it. While he was their captive, he joked with them and even told them he would come back to teach them a lesson. After he was freed, Caesar kept his promise and made sure the pirates were caught and punished.

Mesopotamia
The First Civilization

Mesopotamia is here

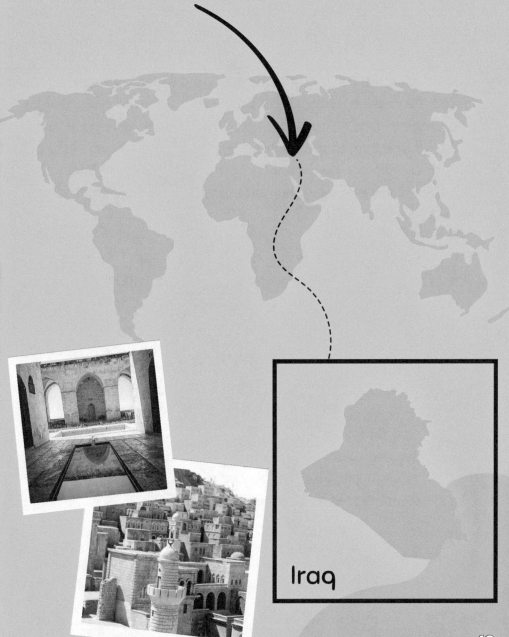

Iraq

The Start of Cities: Sumer and Babylon

The ancient land of Mesopotamia, called the "land between the rivers," was where some of the first cities in the world were built. This land was between the Tigris and Euphrates Rivers, in what is now Iraq. Two of the most important cities were Sumer and Babylon.

Sumer: The people of Sumer were among the first to build cities, around 4000 BC. They created city-states, which were cities that acted like small countries with their own rulers and gods. One of the biggest cities was Uruk, which had high walls and busy markets. The Sumerians invented one of the first writing systems, called cuneiform, by pressing symbols into clay. They also invented the wheel, used plows for farming, and built tall temples called ziggurats.

Babylon: After Sumer, Babylon became powerful and famous. Around 1792 BC, King Hammurabi ruled Babylon and made one of the first sets of written laws, called the Code of Hammurabi. These laws helped keep order in the city. Babylon was known for its wealth, learning, and amazing buildings. The Hanging Gardens of Babylon were said to be beautiful gardens with trees and plants, and they were one of the Seven Wonders of the Ancient World.

Sumer and Babylon helped create what we think of as cities today. They had governments, religions, and busy marketplaces. Their inventions and ideas influenced many other civilizations and are still remembered as important parts of history.

Cuneiform and the First Books

Cuneiform was one of the earliest systems of writing in the world, invented by the Sumerians in Mesopotamia around 3200 BC. The name "cuneiform" comes from the Latin word cuneus, meaning "wedge," because the writing was made up of wedge-shaped marks. Scribes used a tool called a stylus, made from a reed, to press these symbols into soft clay tablets. Once the tablets dried, the writing became permanent.

Cuneiform was used to record many things, from trade and taxes to stories and songs. At first, it was made up of simple pictographs, where each symbol represented an object or idea, like grain or cattle. Over time, the symbols became more abstract and complex, allowing scribes to write more detailed messages.

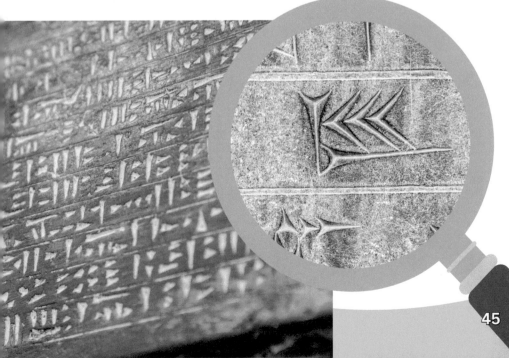

One of the most famous stories written in cuneiform is the Epic of Gilgamesh, one of the oldest known stories in the world. It tells the adventures of King Gilgamesh and explores themes of friendship, heroism, and the search for eternal life. This epic was recorded on clay tablets and is considered one of the first "books" ever created.

Cuneiform allowed civilizations like Sumer and Babylon to keep records, share knowledge, and pass down stories and traditions through generations. This invention laid the groundwork for future writing systems and is an essential part of how humans began to share ideas in a permanent form.

FUN FACT

The Sumerians used cuneiform not only for serious records like laws and trade but also for more fun things—like writing down jokes and riddles! Some of the earliest examples of humor in history were found on cuneiform tablets, showing that even thousands of years ago, people enjoyed telling jokes and having fun.

Gods and Legends: Gilgamesh and the Lives of Kings

The ancient Mesopotamians loved to tell stories about their gods and heroes, and one of their most famous tales is about Gilgamesh, a legendary king. The story of Gilgamesh, written in cuneiform on clay tablets, is one of the oldest stories in the world and shows what the people of ancient times believed and valued.

Who Was Gilgamesh? Gilgamesh was the king of Uruk, a powerful city in Sumer. He wasn't just an ordinary king—legends say he was two-thirds god and one-third human. Gilgamesh was strong and wise but could be proud and sometimes mean. To teach him a lesson, the gods sent Enkidu, a wild man who became Gilgamesh's best friend.

Together, Gilgamesh and Enkidu went on exciting adventures, fighting monsters like Humbaba and the Bull of Heaven. But when Enkidu died, Gilgamesh was very sad and set out on a journey to find the secret to living forever. Along the way, he learned important lessons about life and what it means to be human.

Kings in Mesopotamia were seen as powerful leaders who had the favor of the gods. Temples were built in their honor, and they often played a key role in religious ceremonies. Kings like Hammurabi of Babylon, who created the famous Code of Hammurabi, were celebrated for their wisdom and efforts to bring justice and order to their people. They were not only warriors but also builders of cities, temples, and impressive structures.

The stories of kings like Gilgamesh mixed history with myth, showing that rulers were believed to have special relationships with the gods. These tales were meant to inspire people, teach lessons about bravery and leadership, and remind them that even the most powerful kings faced challenges and sought answers about life and death.

The legends of Gilgamesh and the stories of kings helped shape the culture and beliefs of ancient Mesopotamia, leaving behind a legacy that continues to capture the imagination of people today.

The Tower of Babel and the Hanging Gardens

Ancient Mesopotamia was full of incredible stories and legendary structures, and two of the most famous are the Tower of Babel and the Hanging Gardens of Babylon.

The Tower of Babel: The story of the Tower of Babel comes from the Bible but is connected to the great ziggurats of Mesopotamia. According to the story, people in the city of Babylon wanted to build a tower so tall that it would reach the heavens. This tower symbolized their pride and desire to make a name for themselves. However, God saw their ambition and decided to stop them by confusing their language so they could no longer understand each other. This event led to the people scattering across the Earth and the building of the tower being abandoned.

The story is used to explain why there are so many different languages in the world and serves as a reminder of the limits of human ambition.

The Hanging Gardens of Babylon:

Unlike the Tower of Babel, which is more of a legend, the Hanging Gardens were one of the Seven Wonders of the Ancient World. These beautiful terraced gardens were said to have been built by King Nebuchadnezzar II around 600 BC to please his wife, who missed the green hills of her homeland.

The gardens were described as having lush plants, trees, and flowers that seemed to hang from the terraces, creating a magical, green mountain in the middle of the city. Water was said to flow down through the terraces, using an early form of irrigation to keep the plants healthy in the hot climate.

Although historians have debated whether the gardens truly existed or were just a legend, the story of the Hanging Gardens showcases the creativity and ambition of ancient Babylon. The Tower of Babel and the Hanging Gardens both capture the imagination, showing how the people of Mesopotamia dreamed of reaching the sky and creating beauty that would be remembered for generations.

This is how the Hanging Gardens might have looked back then.

Write Your Own Message in Cuneiform!

Cuneiform was one of the first writing systems in the world, created by the Sumerians. They used wedge-shaped symbols pressed into clay tablets to write messages, keep records, and tell stories. Now, it's your turn to become an ancient scribe!

Instructions:

1. Create Your Tablet: Draw a rectangle on a piece of paper or use modeling clay to create your own "tablet" shape.
2. Choose Your Symbols: Use simple triangle and line shapes to create cuneiform-style marks. You can decide what each symbol means, such as a star for "friend" or a triangle for "home."
3. Write a Short Message: Think of a simple message you want to write, like "Hello" or "I am brave." Use your cuneiform symbols to write it on your "tablet."
4. Decorate Your Tablet: Add patterns or designs around your cuneiform message to make it look more like an ancient clay tablet.
5. Show Your Work: Share your cuneiform message with friends or family and see if they can guess what it says!

This activity will help you understand how early writing worked and give you a taste of what it was like to be a scribe in ancient Mesopotamia. Have fun creating your own secret message in the style of the Sumerians!

The Chinese Inventors and Thinkers

China is here

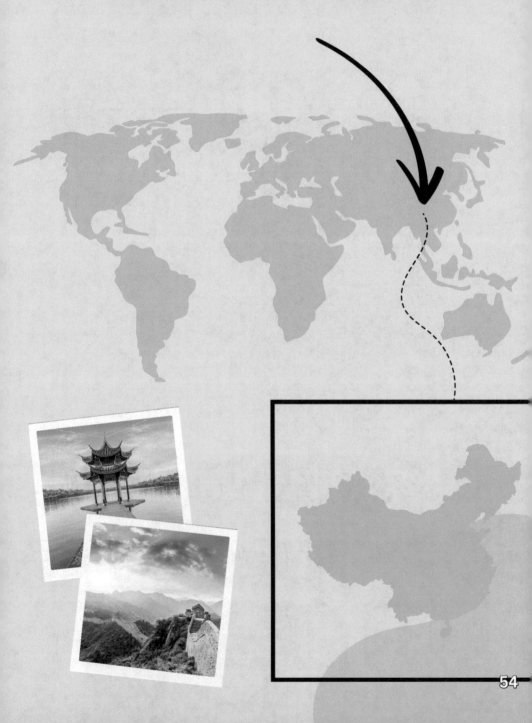

The Middle Kingdom: Emperors and the Great Wall

Ancient China, often called the "Middle Kingdom," was one of the greatest and longest-lasting civilizations in history. The Chinese believed their land was at the center of the world, surrounded by mountains, deserts, and seas that made it both protected and unique. Life in ancient China was ruled by powerful emperors who made important decisions for their people and built incredible structures, the most famous being the Great Wall of China.

The Great Wall: The Great Wall of China is one of the most impressive structures ever built. It was created to protect China from invasions by nomadic tribes from the north. The construction of the wall began as early as the 7th century BC, but it was Emperor Qin Shi Huang who connected and expanded different parts of the wall to create a massive barrier.

The wall stretched for thousands of miles, winding over mountains, deserts, and plains. It was built by soldiers, peasants, and prisoners who worked in difficult conditions to complete the project. The Great Wall not only kept invaders out but also helped control trade along the Silk Road and showed the emperor's power.

Emperors: The emperors of China were like kings but with even more power. They were considered to have a divine right to rule, meaning they were chosen by the heavens. One of the most famous emperors was Qin Shi Huang, the first emperor to unite China.

He created the Qin Dynasty and was known for standardizing money, measurements, and writing across the land, which helped make China stronger and more organized. Emperors lived in grand palaces and were surrounded by advisors and soldiers. They were responsible for the safety of the people, making laws, and expanding their empire.

The emperors and the Great Wall show the strength and big ideas of ancient China. The wall still stands today as a reminder of the hard work and cleverness of the people who built it. The stories of the emperors and their achievements are still an important part of Chinese history and culture.

The Silk Road: How Did Silk Reach Europe?

The Silk Road was not just one road, but a group of trade routes that connected ancient China to Europe and other parts of Asia. It was important for sharing goods, ideas, and cultures across many miles. One of the most valuable things traded on the Silk Road was silk, a beautiful fabric that was very special in the ancient world.

The Secret of Silk: The Chinese discovered how to make silk over 4,000 years ago. They raised silkworms and carefully unwound their cocoons to make fine threads. For a long time, the way to make silk was a secret, and only emperors and rich people could wear it. Silk was a sign of wealth and power.

Silk was carried from China along the Silk Road, which crossed deserts, mountains, and many cities. Merchants traveled in groups with camels or horses, carrying silk and other valuable items like spices and jade. The journey was hard and dangerous, but selling silk in faraway markets brought great rewards.

Silkworm cocoon

Silk in Europe: When silk reached Europe, people were amazed by its softness and shine. The Romans loved silk and used it for clothes and decorations. Even though the secret of making silk eventually spread, China was the main source for a long time.

The Silk Road was more than just a way to trade goods; it was a connection between different parts of the world. It helped spread ideas and cultures, making the world more connected and setting the stage for global trade as we know it today.

Even today, silk remains one of the most luxurious and expensive fabrics in the world. Modern silk is still produced using techniques that are very similar to those used thousands of years ago in ancient China. Countries like China and India are still among the largest producers of silk, continuing a tradition that has lasted for millennia.

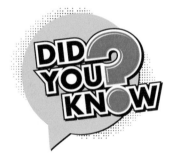

Silk cloth

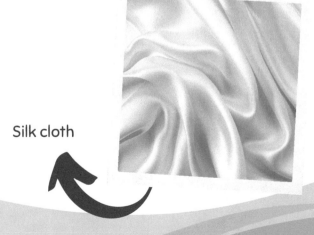

Chinese Inventions: Paper, Compass, and Fireworks

Ancient China was a place of great innovation, and many of its inventions changed the world. Among these were paper, the compass, and fireworks, each of which had a big impact on how people lived and explored.

Paper: Before the invention of paper, people wrote on materials like bamboo, silk, or even animal bones, which were expensive and hard to use. Around 105 AD, Cai Lun, a Chinese official, developed the first true paper using mulberry bark, old rags, and water. This invention made writing and keeping records much easier and cheaper. The use of paper spread slowly at first but eventually reached other parts of the world, transforming communication, art, and learning.

Compass: The ancient Chinese were the first to invent the compass, a tool that changed how people traveled. As early as the 2nd century BC, they found that a special rock called lodestone, which is naturally magnetic, would always point north and south when floating in water or hanging freely.

By the 11th century, during the Song Dynasty, the Chinese made a better version using a magnetized needle. This compass helped sailors find their way, even when the sun or stars were not visible. Later, the compass made its way to Europe and helped start the Age of Exploration, allowing ships to travel farther and discover new places.

Fireworks: Fireworks were invented in China around the 7th century during the Tang Dynasty. The Chinese discovered that mixing saltpeter, sulfur, and charcoal made gunpowder, which would explode when lit. They put this gunpowder into bamboo tubes to create the first simple fireworks. These fireworks were used in celebrations and to scare away evil spirits.

Over time, fireworks became more colorful and exciting, and they spread to other countries, where they are now used in festivals and shows.

The inventions of the ancient Chinese, like paper, the compass, and fireworks, show how creative they were. These inventions changed the way people communicated, traveled, and celebrated, not just in China but all around the world.

Wisdom and Legends

Ancient China was not only known for its incredible inventions but also for its rich traditions, wisdom, and legends. Two important aspects of Chinese culture were the teachings of Confucius and the stories of dragons.

Dragons: In ancient Chinese culture, dragons were powerful and wise creatures, very different from the fire-breathing monsters often seen in Western stories.

Chinese dragons were seen as symbols of strength, luck, and protection. They were believed to control the weather, especially rain, and were often connected to rivers and water. Emperors were thought to be like dragons, as they were considered powerful and able to bring prosperity to the land.

During festivals, like the famous Dragon Boat Festival, people celebrate with dragon-shaped boats and dances, showing how deeply dragons are rooted in Chinese culture.

FAMOUS

Confucius, the Wise Teacher of China

Confucius was a famous and wise teacher who lived in ancient China over 2,500 years ago. He loved to learn and teach others about being kind, fair, and respectful. Confucius believed that people should always try to do the right thing and treat others with kindness.

He taught that families are very important and that children should respect their parents and elders. Confucius also said that leaders should be good and fair to their people, and that this would make the whole country better. Many of his ideas are written down in a book called the Analects, which people still read today.

Confucius's teachings helped shape Chinese culture and are still followed by many people around the world. He is remembered as a great thinker who taught that living a good life means being honest, respectful, and caring towards others.

Coloring Page

The Maya - Secrets of the Rainforest

The Maya lived here

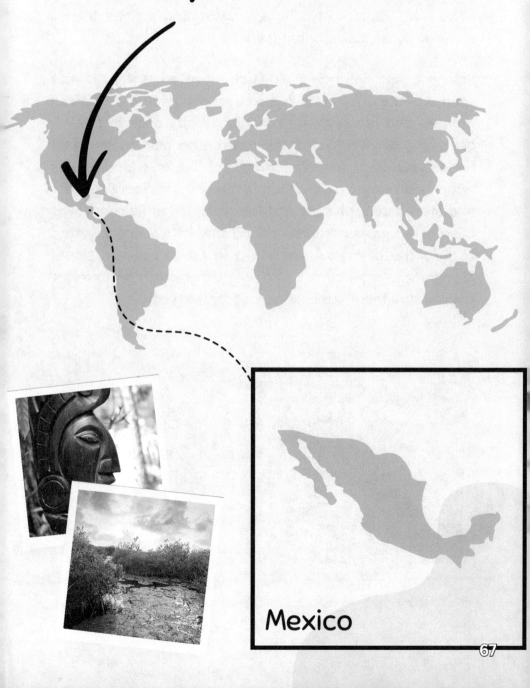

Mexico

Life in the Cities of Pyramids

The ancient Maya civilization thrived in Central America, and two of their most impressive cities were Palenque and Tikal. These cities were centers of culture, religion, and politics, filled with stunning pyramids and vibrant life.

Palenque was an ancient Maya city located in what is now southern Mexico. It was famous for its beautifully carved temples and artwork. The city reached its peak in the 7th century under King Pakal the Great, who built many of its famous buildings, like the Temple of the Inscriptions. This temple also served as King Pakal's tomb and had carvings that told stories about his life and the gods. Life in Palenque was busy, with farmers, craftsmen, and traders working together to help the city grow. The Maya in Palenque were skilled farmers who grew corn, beans, and other crops on terraces, making sure there was enough food for everyone.

Tikal: Tikal, located in present-day Guatemala, was one of the biggest and most powerful Maya cities. Its tall pyramids stood high above the thick jungle, and one of its most famous buildings was the Great Jaguar Temple. Tikal was a center for politics, trade, and religion, attracting people from all around.

The city had a complex society. Nobles, priests, and rulers were at the top, while farmers, craftsmen, and workers made up most of the population. The rulers of Tikal were strong in battle and often competed with nearby cities to stay in power.

Daily life in Maya cities was centered around the sun, seasons, and religious ceremonies. The Maya believed that their gods controlled nature and life, so they built large temples and held rituals to honor them. Priests were very important because they understood the wishes of the gods and performed ceremonies to keep the city in harmony with nature and the spiritual world.

Maya Calendar and Astronomy: How the Maya Saw the Stars

The ancient Maya civilization was not only known for its impressive cities and pyramids but also for its incredible knowledge of astronomy and timekeeping. The Maya looked to the stars to guide their lives, plan their activities, and understand the world around them. Their advanced understanding of the night sky led them to create one of the most sophisticated calendar systems in the ancient world.

The Maya Calendar: The Maya had more than one calendar, each serving a different purpose. The Tzolk'in, or Sacred Round, was a 260-day calendar used for religious and ceremonial events. It was made up of 20 periods, each with 13 days. The Haab', or solar calendar, had 365 days, similar to the one we use today.

It was divided into 18 months of 20 days each, plus an extra short month of 5 "nameless" days that were considered unlucky. Together, these calendars formed the Calendar Round, which repeated every 52 years. The Maya also developed the Long Count Calendar, which was used to mark longer periods of time and significant historical events. This calendar kept track of years in cycles that lasted over 5,000 years.

Astronomy and Star Watching: The Maya were expert astronomers. They built observatories and positioned their temples to align with the movements of the sun, moon, and planets.

This careful observation allowed them to predict solar eclipses and track the cycles of Venus, which played an important role in their mythology and timing of events. The knowledge they gathered helped them plan when to plant crops, hold religious ceremonies, and celebrate festivals.

For example, the pyramid at Chichen Itza, known as El Castillo, was designed so that during the spring and fall equinoxes, a shadow in the shape of a serpent appeared on its steps, a nod to the god Kukulkan.

Understanding the Universe: The Maya saw the sky as more than just stars and planets; they believed it was the home of gods and powerful spirits.

Their myths included stories of creation and cosmic battles that influenced the world below. The Maya believed that the movements of the celestial bodies were messages from the gods, and they recorded these movements in detailed codices—folded books made of bark paper. Unfortunately, only a few of these codices have survived, but they give us a glimpse into how advanced and precise Maya astronomy was.

The Maya's deep understanding of calendars and astronomy helped them organize their society and connect with the spiritual world. Their legacy shows that they were not only skilled builders and artists but also brilliant scientists who mapped the heavens with incredible accuracy.

Writing and Numbers: The Mystery of Maya Script

The ancient Maya developed one of the most complex writing systems in the ancient world, known as Maya script or Maya hieroglyphs. This system, along with their advanced understanding of numbers, allowed them to record their history, religious beliefs, and important events in great detail. The Maya's writing and number system continue to fascinate historians and archaeologists today.

Maya Script: The Maya script was a combination of symbols called glyphs, which could represent words, sounds, or ideas. Each glyph was highly detailed and could be combined in different ways to create sentences and convey complex meanings.

These glyphs were carved into stone monuments, painted on pottery, and written in codices (folded books made from bark paper). The script was used by scribes, who were highly respected in Maya society and often worked for kings or temples to record important events such as battles, royal ceremonies, and religious stories.

Deciphering the Maya script was a mystery for many years because the language was lost after the Spanish conquest in the 16th century. Only a few codices survived, as many were destroyed during that time. However, thanks to the work of modern archaeologists and linguists, much of the Maya writing has been decoded, revealing a rich history and culture full of stories about their gods, rulers, and daily life.

Numbers and Math: The Maya also had a sophisticated number system that included the concept of zero, a mathematical idea that many ancient civilizations did not use. Their number system was based on 20 (a vigesimal system) instead of the base 10 system we use today. Maya numbers were represented by dots, bars, and a special symbol for zero that looked like a shell. With this system, they could perform complex calculations, which helped them create their detailed calendar and track astronomical events with great precision.

The Maya used their knowledge of numbers not just for counting but for planning religious ceremonies and building their impressive structures. Temples and pyramids were often aligned with astronomical events and built with a number of steps or levels that reflected important numbers in their culture, such as 260 (the number of days in the Tzolk'in calendar).

The script and number system of the Maya demonstrate their intelligence and creativity. These tools allowed them to leave a written record of their civilization that still speaks to us today, offering insights into how they lived, what they valued, and how they saw the world.

Gods and Rituals: Religion and Traditions of the Maya

The ancient Maya civilization was deeply spiritual, with a rich and complex religion that influenced nearly every aspect of their daily life. They believed that their world was filled with gods and powerful spirits who controlled nature, the weather, and even their fate. To keep the gods happy and maintain balance in the universe, the Maya performed many rituals and ceremonies.

The Gods: The Maya pantheon included many gods, each with specific powers and responsibilities. Some of the most important gods were Itzamna, the creator god and ruler of the heavens; Chaac, the god of rain who was essential for crops and agriculture; and Kukulkan, the feathered serpent deity who symbolized both water and wind and was central to myths and rituals. The Maya believed that these gods could be kind or angry, so keeping them pleased was vital for a good harvest, protection, and prosperity.

Rituals and Ceremonies: To honor their gods, the Maya held elaborate rituals that often involved music, dance, and offerings. These ceremonies were performed by priests and sometimes the rulers, who acted as intermediaries between the people and the gods.

The Maya made special offerings to honor their gods. These offerings could include food, precious stones, or jade. They believed that giving something valuable, like food or beautiful stones, would please the gods and bring blessings like rain, good health, or success in battle. In important ceremonies, priests and rulers made these offerings to show respect and keep their people safe.

The Maya believed in an afterlife, a place people went after they died. They thought that reaching this peaceful place could be challenging. Certain people, like warriors who died in battle, went straight to a heavenly paradise. Others had to pass through a place called Xibalba, the underworld, where they faced tests from different gods.

The Maya's rituals and traditions show their deep respect for the gods and nature. By performing these ceremonies and building grand temples, the Maya showed their devotion and hoped to keep harmony with the powerful forces they believed in.

What We Can Learn from Ancient Civilizations

What Did the Ancient World Leave Us?

The ancient world gave us many things that we still use and learn from today. From the huge pyramids of Egypt to the wise ideas of Greek philosophers, ancient civilizations helped shape the world as we know it. Here are some of the most important things the ancient world gave us:

- Buildings and Inventions: The Egyptians, Greeks, and Romans built amazing structures like the pyramids, the Parthenon, and the Great Wall of China. Their ideas about building and engineering still inspire architects today. Modern bridges, roads, and buildings often use techniques invented thousands of years ago.

- Writing and Stories: Ancient people invented ways to write so they could keep records and tell stories. The Sumerians created one of the first writing systems, called cuneiform, while the Egyptians used hieroglyphics. Thanks to these early writings, we know about stories like the Epic of Gilgamesh and Homer's Iliad. Writing helps us share ideas, just like it did in ancient times.

- Laws and Government: The Greeks and Romans introduced the idea of democracy, where people have a say in government. Ancient Babylon had one of the first sets of laws, the Code of Hammurabi. These early ideas about fairness and justice still influence our modern governments.

- Science and Math: The Egyptians used math to build their pyramids, and the Greeks, like Pythagoras, made discoveries in geometry. The Maya created a complex calendar based on their understanding of the stars. These contributions are the basis for much of modern science and math.

- Art and Culture: Ancient people made beautiful statues, paintings, and pottery that showed their beliefs and everyday life. The Greeks also developed theater, which we still enjoy today. Their creativity in art and culture continues to inspire artists and performers.

The ancient world gave us more than just old buildings and stories. It provided the foundation for many parts of our modern life. By studying these ancient civilizations, we can learn important lessons about creativity, knowledge, and working together.

A Journey to the Past and the Future

Exploring the ancient world is like stepping into a time machine that takes us back to the very beginning. The past is filled with stories of great leaders, wise thinkers, talented artists, and everyday people who helped build the civilizations we admire today. Each discovery, like a forgotten city, an old temple, or a piece of ancient writing, is like finding a clue about who we are and where we come from.

Learning about the past isn't just about old events; it's about connecting those lessons to today and tomorrow. The amazing achievements of the Egyptians with the pyramids, the democratic ideas of the Greeks, and the clever engineering of the Romans show us what people can create when they work together. These stories remind us that people have always used their creativity and determination to build great things.

As we learn from these ancient civilizations, we can be inspired to make new advancements ourselves. Modern builders still admire the balance of Greek temples, and scientists look back at the discoveries of the Maya and Mesopotamians in math and astronomy. Even things we use every day, like our calendar, come from ancient ideas.

Understanding ancient civilizations helps us see our world as part of a much bigger story—one that started long before us and will continue long after. By respecting and learning from the past, we build a bridge to the future.

So, as we look forward, we can use the wisdom, creativity, and lessons from the ancient world to shape a future that is just as bold and inspiring. The past may be ancient, but its legacy is still with us, guiding us as we explore and write the next chapters of our story.

THANK YOU FOR EXPLORING

We hope you enjoyed this journey through the ancient world! Exploring the stories of great civilizations, amazing inventions, wise leaders, and fascinating cultures helps us understand just how incredible our shared history is. Each story and discovery gives us a glimpse into the lives of people who lived thousands of years ago, yet whose ideas, creativity, and courage still shape our world today.

If you want to learn even more, there are many ways to continue exploring! Check out books about ancient Egypt, Greece, Rome, and China at your local library, or look for documentaries and kid-friendly websites that bring ancient history to life with exciting facts, pictures, and videos. Some museums even have online exhibits where you can explore ancient artifacts from home.

The adventure doesn't have to end here. The ancient world has so much to teach us, and the more we learn, the more we can appreciate the amazing achievements of those who came before us.

Thanks for joining this journey!

QUIZ TIME!

Have fun checking your answers and seeing how much you know about the ancient world!

1. Where was the first writing developed?
- □ a) Egypt
- □ b) Rome
- □ c) Mesopotamia

2. What was the most important river in ancient Egypt?
- □ a) The Ganges
- □ b) The Nile
- □ c) The Amazon

3. Who was the last ruler of ancient Egypt?
- □ a) Ramses II
- □ b) Tutankhamun
- □ c) Cleopatra

4. What is the famous Greek story about a hero's adventures?
- □ a) The Odyssey
- □ b) The Bible
- □ c) The Epic of Gilgamesh

5. What was first invented in China?
- □ a) The compass
- □ b) The telephone
- □ c) Printing

6. What was developed in the city of Babylon to organize society?
- ☐ a) Democracy
- ☐ b) The Code of Hammurabi
- ☐ c) Mathematics

7. Who was the famous teacher of wisdom in China?
- ☐ a) Socrates
- ☐ b) Confucius
- ☐ c) Julius Caesar

8. What was the role of Maya priests?
- ☐ a) To harvest crops
- ☐ b) To honor the gods and perform rituals
- ☐ c) To train soldiers

9. Why was the Silk Road important?
- ☐ a) It was a trade route connecting China and Europe
- ☐ b) It was a famous river in Greece
- ☐ c) It led to the discovery of America

10. What was the Romans' most important achievement in architecture?
- ☐ a) Skyscrapers
- ☐ b) Pyramids
- ☐ c) Aqueducts

 Answers:

10.c) Aqueducts
9.a) It was a trade route connecting China and Europe
8.b) To honor the gods and perform rituals
7.b) Confucius
6.b) The Code of Hammurabi
5.a) The compass
4.a) The Odyssey
3.c) Cleopatra
2.b) The Nile
1.c) Mesopotamia

IMPRINT

Information according to § 5 TMG:
Markus Gohlke
c/o IP-Management #16265
Ludwig-Erhard-Str. 18
20459 Hamburg
Contact:
E-mail: elcamondobeach@gmail.com
Phone: +491751555847
Imprint: Independently published

Made in United States
Troutdale, OR
12/08/2024

26097223R00049